The
Discover
Art
Program

Adventures in Art

Laura H. Chapman

Davis Publications, Inc.   Worcester, Massachusetts

Printed in the United States of America
ISBN: 87192-252-5

10 9 8 7 6 5 4 3 2 1

Cover, top right: Unknown, Head of Sasanian King Shapur II. Silver. Metropolitan Museum of Art, New York. **Top left:** Albert Dumouchel, Still Life, 1946. Oil on pane, 30 1/2 x 26" (77 x 65 cm). National Bank of Canada, Montreal. **Bottom:** Student artwork.

Back cover, top: Unknown, Late Classic Serape, ca. 1870. Raveled flannel and bayeta field, indigo blue, anilin yellow, 52 1/2 x 68 3/4" (133 x 175 cm). Hozho' Gallery, Crested Butte, Colorado.

Title page: Vincent Van Gogh, The Garden of the Poets, 1988. Oil on canvas, 28 3/4 x 36 1/4" (73 x 92 cm). ©1991 The Art Institute of Chicago, All Rights Reserved (Mr. and Mrs. Lewis L. Coburn Memorial Collection).

Editorial Advisory Board:

Dr. Cynthia Colbert
Chair of the Art Education Dept.,
Professor of Art
University of South Carolina
Columbia, South Carolina

Bill MacDonald
Art Education Consultant
Vancouver, British Columbia
Canada

Dr. Connie Newton
Assistant Professor of Art
School of Visual Art
University of North Texas
Denton, Texas

Sandra Noble
Curriculum Specialist for the Fine Arts
Cleveland Public Schools
Cleveland, Ohio

Reading Consultant:

Dr. JoAnn Canales
College of Art Education
University of North Texas
Denton, Texas

Reviewers:

Cliff Cousins
Art Specialist
Davenport Community School District
Davenport, Iowa

Dr. Lila G. Crespin
College of Fine Art
California State University at
Long Beach

Lee Gage
Art Supervisor
Westchester Area School District
Westchester, Pennsylvania

William Gay, Jr.
Visual Art Coordinator
Richland County School District One
Columbia, South Carolina

Dr. Adrienne W. Hoard
Associate Professor
University of Missouri-Columbia

Mary Jordan
Visual Arts Curriculum Specialist
Tempe, Arizona

Kathleen Lockhart
Curriculum & Instructional Specialist
Baltimore, Maryland

David McIntyre
Consultant for Visual Arts
El Paso Independent School District
El Paso, Texas

R. Barry Shauck
Supervisor of Art
Howard County Public School
Ellicott City, Maryland

Linda Sleight
Visual Arts Curriculum Specialist
Tempe, Arizona

Carl Yochum
Director Fine Arts
Ferguson-Florissant School District
Florrisant, Missouri

Joyce Young
Assistant Principal
Bond Hill School
Cincinnati, Ohio

Acknowledgements:
The author and publisher would like to thank the following individuals and groups for their special assistance in providing images, resources and other help: Tom Feelings, Mickey Ford, Claire Mowbray Golding, Colleen Kelley, Samella Lewis, Maya Nigrosh, Sandra Palmer, Dawn Reddy, Tara Reddy, Patricia A. Renick, Chloe Sayer, Martha Siegel, Martin Speed, Bernice Steinbaum, Anne Straus, and art teachers in the Department of Defense Dependent Schools.

Managing Editor:
Wyatt Wade

Editor:
Laura J. Marshall

Design:
Douglass Scott, WGBH Design

Production:
Nancy Dutting

Photo Acquisitions:
Allan Harper

Illustrator:
Susan Christy-Pallo

Photography:
Schlowsky Photography

Contents

Can you see your world as **artists** do?

Artists look for colors, lines and shapes.

They see textures and spaces, too.

6

Photograph: Mickey Ford.

Can you find art in nature?

Can you find art in the things people make?

What kind of art do you like to see? Why?

What kind of art do you like to create? Why?

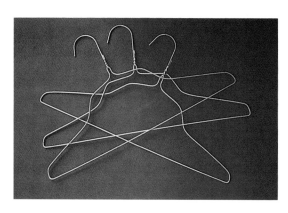

You can see your world like an artist.

Look at the photographs on this page.

The artists saw **lines** in nature.

The artists saw lines in things people use.

Lines can be thick or thin, long or short.

Lines can be curved or straight.

Have you seen wavy or zigzag lines?

 Ruth Takubo, *Study: Tree,* 1991. Ink on paper, 6 3/4 x 10 5/8 " (27 x 116 cm). Courtesy of the artist.

 Chin Nung, *Blossoming Plum,* 1760. Hanging scroll, ink and light color on paper. The Nelson-Atkins Museum of Art, Kansas City, Missouri (Nelson Fund).

Look at the artworks in pictures E and F.

How are the lines alike? How are they different?

Draw a picture of your favorite tree.

What lines will you use?

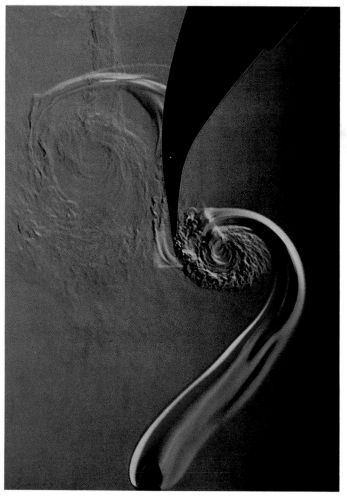

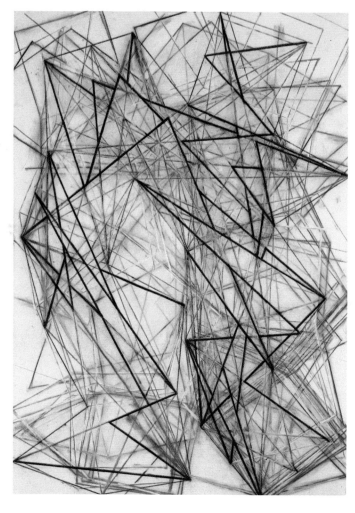

 A **Harold Edgerton,** *Fan Blade Vortex,* 1973. Color
photographic print, 19 15/16 x 14 1/8" (51 x 36 cm). Spencer
Museum of Art, University of Kansas (Gift of Gus & Arlette
Kayafas).

B **Mel Bochner,** *Vertigo,* 1982. Charcoal, conte crayon and
pastel on paper, 108 x 74" (274 x 188 cm). Albright-Knox Art
Gallery, Buffalo, New York (Charles Clifton Fund).

Lines can show **motion.**

Lines can give you feelings of motion.

Look at pictures A and B.

What motions do you see and feel? Why?

Katsushika Hokusai, *The Great Wave at Kanagawa,* 1823-29. Woodblock print, 10 1/8" x 14 15/16" (26 x 38 cm). The Metropolitan Museum of Art (Bequest of Mrs. H. O. Havemeyer, 1929. The H. O. Havemeyer Collection).

An artist from Japan created this artwork.

What lines help you see the motion?

Can you feel the motion too?

Think about things that move.

Draw lines that show how they move.

3 Shapes Express Feelings
A Collage of a Face

 Paul Klee, *Arab Song,* 1932. Gouache on unprimed burlap, 35 7/8 x 25 1/2" (91 x 65 cm). © The Phillips Collection, Washington, DC (Acquired from Karl Nierendorf, New York, 1941).

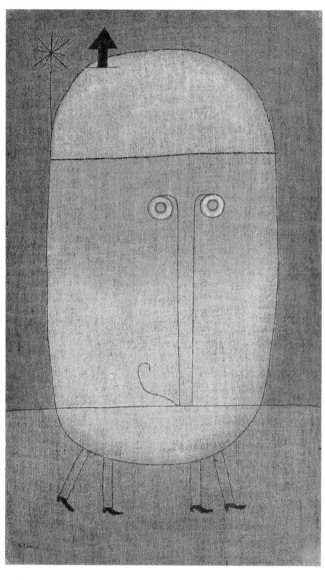

 Paul Klee, *Mask of Fear,* 1932. Oil on burlap, 39 1/2 x 22 1/2" (100 x 57 cm). Collection, The Museum of Modern Art, New York (Purchase).

Look at pictures A, B and C. One artist created these artworks.
What **shapes** are the faces?

What feeling does each artwork show?
How does the artist show this feeling?

Paul Klee, *Senecio,* 1922. Oil on
linen, 16 x 15" (41 x 38 cm).
Kunstmuseum, Basel, Switzerland.

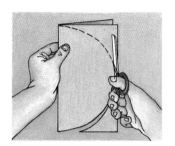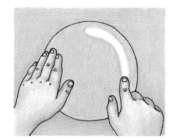

Fold paper.

Cut a big shape for the face.

Paste the edges neatly.

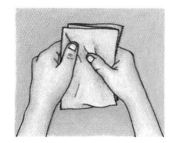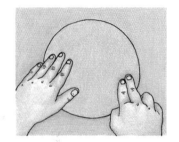

Wipe paste from your hands.
Press the shape down. Cut
and paste other shapes.
What else can you add?

Create a **collage** of a face.
Plan your collage of a face.
What feeling will you show?
How will you show it?

(A)

(B)

You feel a **texture** when you touch a surface.

The texture may feel rough or smooth.

It may feel prickly or silky or bumpy.

You can see textures too.

What textures do you see in pictures A and B?

How do you think they feel?

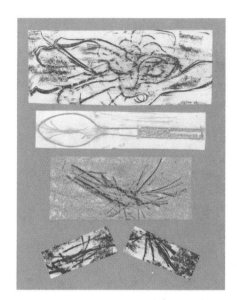

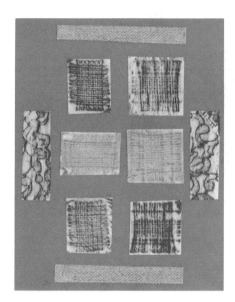

C   **Robert Indiana, *The Great American Dream: New York,*** 1966.
Crayon and frottage on paper, 39 1/2 x 26" (100 x 66 cm).
Collection of Whitney Museum of American Art, New York
(Gift of Norman Dubrow). Photograph: Geoffrey Clements.

Picture C is a texture rubbing of a sign.

The artist put paper over the sign.

He rubbed the paper with a pencil.

What texture rubbings can you create?

 Scene from pedestal of the Wei Dynasty, 524 A.D. Stone (limestone) rubbing from Buddhist stele, 24 1/2 x 19 1/2 x 24 3/4" (62 x 50 x 63 cm). The University Museum, University of Pennsylvania.

Pictures A and B show parades in China.

Each artwork is a **print** made from a carving.

The artist put paper over the carving.

Then the artist rubbed the paper with crayon.

 Ho Huan Tree (detail), 147 A.D. Stone rubbing, 15 1/4 x 28 1/4" (39 x 72 cm). Philadelphia Museum of Art (Given by Horace Jayne).

 Student artwork.

Students made this print from a collage.
They made a rubbing of the collage.
You can make a rubbing from a collage.
Chinese artists invented this way to print.

1. Cut big and little shapes from paper.

2. Glue the big shapes. Put small ones on top.

3. Tape paper down. Rub crayon all over.

A Saul Steinberg, *Joy Continuous Miner,* 1914. Watercolor, pen and ink and paper on paper, 28 x 22" (71 x 56 cm). The Carnegie Museum of Art, Pittsburgh (Gift of Joy Manufacturing Company).

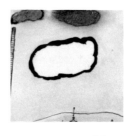

An outline goes around a shape.

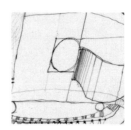

Lines can make many shapes.

Lines can suggest texture.

B

What did this artist show underground?

What do you see above the ground?

Where do you see shapes with outlines?

How did the artist show textures?

What space do you see in picture C?

What do the lines, textures and shapes mean?

Pretend you could dig a giant hole.

What might you see underground?

Make a picture to share your ideas.

These are **prints** of a finger.
The finger had ink on it.

 A

This **pattern** was printed with a piece of wood.
The wood had paint on it.

B

C You can make a print.

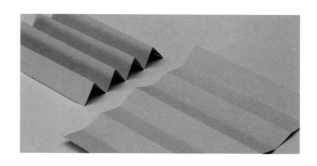

1. Find objects to print.

2. Fold paper. Unfold it.

Artists create repeated patterns.

Some patterns are printed on fabrics.

You can print a repeated pattern on paper.

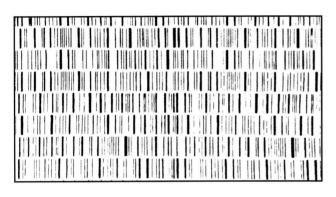

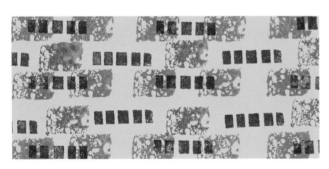

3. Press object on pad.

4. Press. Lift up.

 Rupert Garcia, *Maguey de la Vida,* 1973. Silkscreen, ink on paper, 20 x 26" (51 x 66 cm). Rena Bransten Gallery, San Francisco. Photograph: M. Lee Fatherree, Berkeley, California.

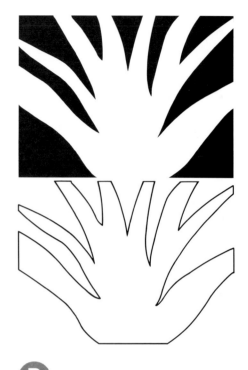 **B**

Artists plan the shapes in their artwork.
You can plan the shapes in your artwork.

Look at the big green plant in picture A.
The green plant is a **positive** shape.
A positive shape is the one you see first.

You can see **negative** shapes in the background.
The negative shapes in picture A are orange.

C **Alexandra Peterson, *Tree Fingers.*** Courtesy of the artist.

D

Look at picture C. Where do you see negative shapes?

What positive shape do you see?

Students created the artwork in pictures E and F.

How did they plan the shapes?

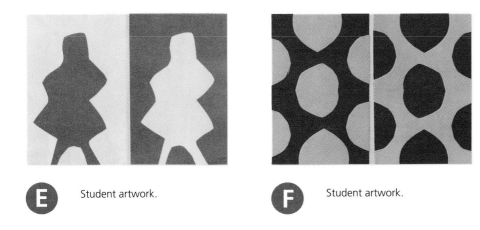

E Student artwork.

F Student artwork.

A　**Henri Matisse, *The Parakeet and the Mermaid*** (detail), 1952.

An artist planned these shapes.

Some of the curved shapes are related, or similar.

They look like a family of shapes.

B

The shapes are printed with **stencils**.

 Student artwork.

Students created stencils. They printed their stencils. You can make a stencil. Then you can print it.

1. Plan a shape for your stencil. Draw and cut it. Can you cut curved shapes?

2. Dab paint inside the stencil. Print the stencil again. Do you know how?

Romare Bearden at work in his studio. Photograph: Frank C. Stewart.

B **Romare Bearden,** ***Eastern Barn,*** 1968. Collage of paper on board, 55 1/2 x 44" (141 x 112 cm). Collection of Whitney Museum of American Art, New York (Purchase 69.14). Photograph: Peter Accettola, Staten Island, New York.

Romare Bearden was an artist.

He made the collage in picture B.

He cut shapes from **photographs** and paper.

He pasted the shapes down to make artwork.

C Student artwork.

E Student artwork.

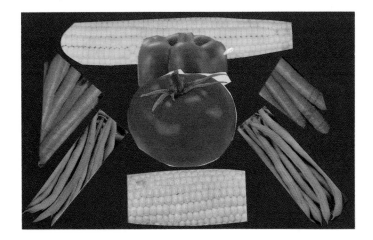

D Student artwork.

Children made these collages.

They cut shapes from old magazines.

How did they plan their artwork?

What kind of collage can you create?

 Torres Garcia, *The Port,* 1942. Oil on cardboard, 31 3/8 x 39 7/8" (80 x 101 cm). Collection, The Museum of Modern Art, New York (Inter-American Fund). Photograph © 1992.

What places in your town do you like to see?

Look at the painting in picture A.

Do you see big and little boats?

What else did the artist show?

Have you ever seen a port in a city?

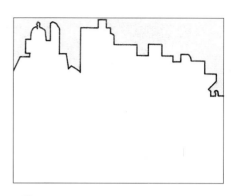

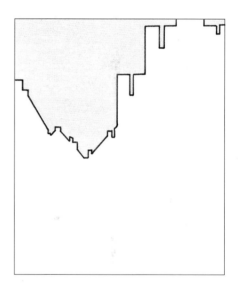

Johannes Vermeer, *Little Street,* 1661. 20 3/4 x 17" (53 x 43 cm). Rijksmuseum, Amsterdam.

This painting was created long ago in Holland.
Have you ever seen a street like this?

What shapes do these paintings have?
What shapes do you see in the buildings?
How did the artists plan a space for the sky?

This is a color wheel.

The arrows show how to mix colors.

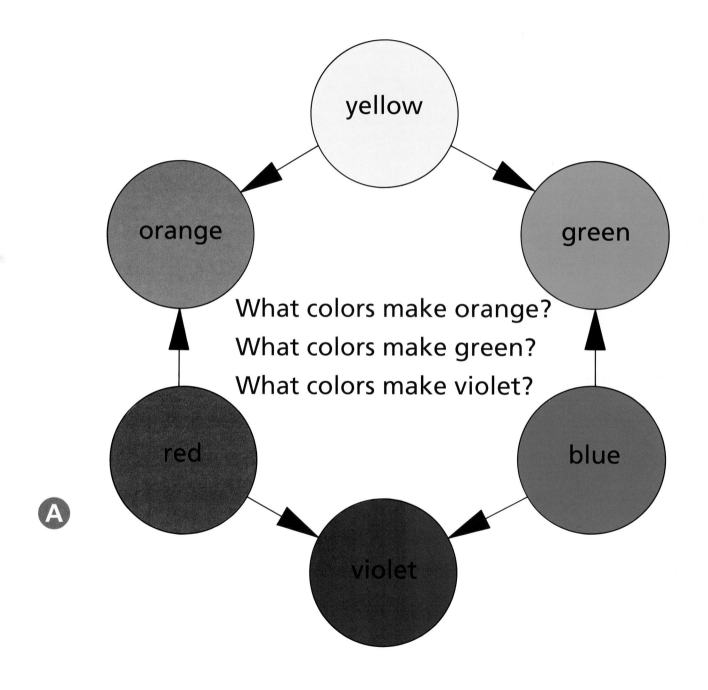

What colors make orange?

What colors make green?

What colors make violet?

Ⓐ

Red, yellow and blue are **primary** colors.

The **secondary** colors are orange, green and violet.

Vincent Van Gogh, *Irises,* 1890. Oil on canvas, 28 x 36 5/8" (71 x 93 cm). The J. Paul Getty Museum, Malibu, California.

Why do you think the artist made this painting?

Where do you see primary and secondary colors?

What other colors do you see?

You can create your own painting.

What colorful things can you show?

There are many ways to use paint.

Some artists want colors to run together.

The colors mix and make soft, fuzzy shapes.

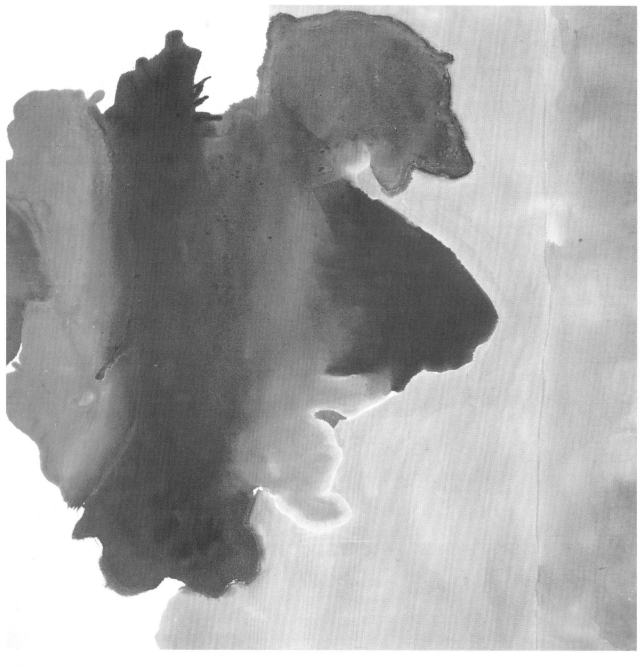

 Helen Frankenthaler, *The Bay,* 1963. Acrylic resin on canvas, 80 3/4 x 81 3/4" (205 x 208 cm). © The Detroit Institute of Arts, 1991 (Gift of Dr. & Mrs. Hilbert H. DeLawter).

You can use paints in many ways.
Create a painting with fuzzy edges.
Let the colors mix and run together.

 Mark Rothko, *No. 18, 1948,* 1949. Oil on canvas, 67 x 56" (170 x 140 cm). Vassar College Art Gallery, Poughkeepsie, New York (Gift of Mrs. John D. Rockefeller III).

 Wassily Kandinsky, *Sketch 1 for Composition VII,* 1913. Oil on canvas, 30 1/4 x 39 3/8" (77 x 98 cm). Städtische Galerie im Lenbachhaus.

Artists use paint in many ways.

They use a **paintbrush** to make colors, lines and shapes.

Someone said this about the painting in picture A:

"Everything is flying through space."

What do you say about this painting?

Look at the big painting.
Find **brushstrokes.**
What else do you see?

You can make a painting.
Remember these steps.
Do you know why?

thick and
thin lines

patches of
color

zigzag and curved lines

dots and wavy lines

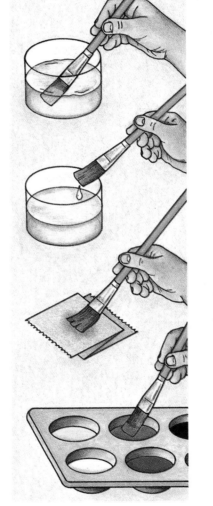

 wash

wipe

blot

next
color

 Deborah Morrissey McGoff, *Day Storm Passing,* 1984. Pastel on paper, 16 x 40" (41 x 102 cm). Courtesy of the artist.

Deborah Morrissey McGoff created these drawings. She has learned to see beauty in nature. Where do you see beauty in nature?

 Deborah Morrissey McGoff, *Afternoon Glaze,* 1983. Acrylic on paper, 30 x 40" (76 x 102 cm). Courtesy of the artist.

Deborah Morrissey McGoff draws many **landscapes.**
She likes to study textures and shapes.
She uses colors to show what she sees.

C Deborah Morrissey McGoff, *Tree Study West/Day,* 1982.
Pastel on paper, 25 x 26" (64 x 66 cm). Courtesy of the artist.

D Deborah Morrissey McGoff, *Myth in Memory,* 1983.
Pastel on paper, 22 1/4 x 26" (57 x 66 cm). Courtesy of the artist.

Look for the plan in each drawing.

Where is the sky?

Where is the ground?

Why does each drawing have a different shape?

What do you like to see outdoors? Why?

What kind of landscape can you draw?

 Leonardo da Vinci, *Studies of Cats and Dragons*, ca. 1513-14. Pen and ink and wash over black chalk, 10 3/8 x 8 1/4" (26 x 21 cm). Windsor Castle, Royal Library © 1992 Her Majesty Queen Elizabeth II.

 Nampahc Arual, *Sketches from Television Imagery*, 1982. Marker, 4 x 8" (10 x 20 cm). Courtesy of the artist.

Sketches are drawings that help you see and think.

Sketches help you remember and imagine things.

Artists made the sketches in pictures A and B.

What did the artists sketch?

Many artists keep sketchbooks.

They fill the blank pages with drawings.

The sketches help them get ideas for art.

C You can make and use a sketchbook.

1. Fold paper for the book.

2. Mark even spaces.

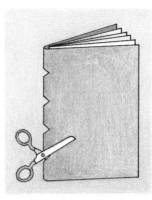

3. Cut out small holes.

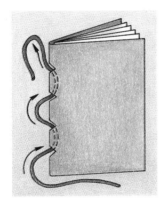

4. Weave yarn in and out.

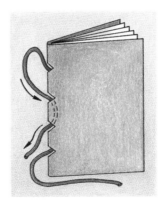

5. Weave again, in and out.

6. Tie a bow or a knot.

D Student artwork.

A   **Thomas Gainsborough, *Six Studies of a Cat.*** Black and white chalk on buff paper, 13 x 17 3/4 " (33 x 45 cm). Rijksmuseum, Amsterdam.

Sketching is a way to learn new things.
Sketching is making drawings for yourself.

The drawings in picture A are sketches.
The artist drew one cat many times.
What did his sketches help him learn?

Student artwork.

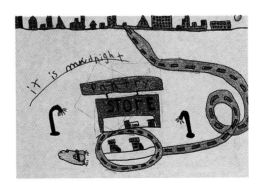

Student artwork.

B **Leonardo da Vinci, *Lily,*** 1475. Pink and brown wash over black chalk-white heightener, 12 x 7" (31 x 17 cm). Windsor Castle, Royal Library © 1992 Her Majesty the Queen.

An artist sketched the lily over 500 years ago.
How can you tell the drawing is a sketch?

Students made the sketches in pictures C and D.
What do their sketches show?
What would you like to sketch? Why?

Warm and Cool Colors
Picturing Places

 James Ensor, *Fireworks,* 1887. Oil and encaustic on canvas, 40 1/4 x 44 1/4 " (102 x 112 cm). Albright-Knox Art Gallery, Buffalo, New York (George B. and Jenny R. Mathews Fund, 1970).

Do you see red, yellow and orange in picture A?

Artists call these **warm colors**.

Why did the artist use warm colors?

Where else do you see colors like these?

B **G.A. Reid,** *The Northern Entrance to Orient Bay, Lake Nipigon,* 1929. 10 x 12″ (25 x 31 cm).
Government of Ontario Art Collection, Toronto. Photograph: Tom Moore Photography, Toronto.

This painting has many blues, greens and violets.

Artists call these **cool colors**.

Where else do you see cool colors?

When might you use warm or cool colors? Why?

 Vincent Van Gogh, *The Garden of the Poets (Le jardin des poètes),* 1888. Oil on canvas, 28 3/4 x 36 1/4″ (73 x 92 cm). ©1991 The Art Institute of Chicago, All Rights Reserved. (Mr. and Mrs. Lewis L. Coburn Memorial Collection).

This painting has many light colors.
It has some dark colors too.
Dark colors are called **shades.**

Why did the artist use light and dark colors?

Have you seen colors like these?
When?

You can mix shades.

B

 Student artwork.

 Claude Monet, _Woman Seated Under the Willows,_ 1880. Oil on linen canvas, 31 7/8 x 23 3/5″ (81 x 60 cm). National Gallery of Art, Washington, DC (Chester Dale Collection).

You can mix tints.

Can you find the light colors?

Light colors are called **tints**.

Why did the artist use many tints?

Have you seen colors like these?

When?

45

 Louis M. Eilshemius, *Approaching Storm,* 1890. Oil on cardboard, 22 5/8 x 26 5/8" (57 x 68 cm).
©The Phillips Collection, Washington, DC.

What happens when a storm comes?

How did this artist plan the sky in his painting?

Why are the fields light and bright?

What else did the artist want you to see?

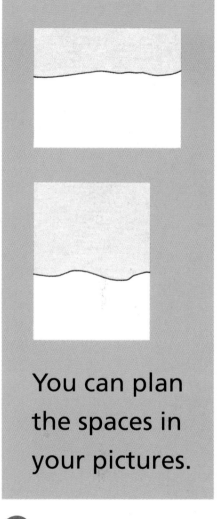

You can plan the spaces in your pictures.

C

What does this artist want you to see and feel?

How does the painting send you messages?

Paint a picture of a stormy day. How will you plan it?

Will you make a tall or a wide painting? Why?

A   **J. Ernest Sampson, *Armistice Day, Toronto,*** ca.1918. Oil on linen, 60 3/8 x 36 1/8" (154 x 92 cm). © Canadian War Museum, Canadian Museum of Civilization. Photograph: William Kent.

B   **Ichiryusai Hiroshige, *Ohashi, Sudden Shower at Atake (Storm on the Great Bridge),*** 1857. Woodblock print. The Toledo Museum of Art, Ohio (Carrie C. Brown Bequest Fund).

How can you show the wind in an artwork?

Study the artworks in this lesson.

Look at the lines, colors and shapes.

How do these artists show the wind?

The wind makes objects move.

You can show motion in many ways.

You can use lines: diagonal, zigzag or wavy.

You can use shapes that slant or bend.

Paint a picture about the wind.

How will your painting show the wind?

Moses Soyer, *Gwen and Jacob Lawrence,* 1962. Oil on canvas, 30 x 36" (76 x 91 cm). Edwin A. Ulrich Museum of Art, The Wichita State University (Endowment Association Art Collection).

A **portrait** is an artwork that shows a real person.
The two people in this portrait are artists.
Their names are Gwen and Jacob Lawrence.

A friend painted this portrait of Mr. and Mrs. Lawrence.
Their friend was an artist. Do you know any artists?

B Marie Louise Elisabeth Vigée-Lebrun, *The Artist's Brother,* 1773. Oil on canvas, 24 x 19" (61 x 48 cm). The Saint Louis Art Museum (Museum Purchase).

C Marie Louise Elisabeth Vigée-Lebrun, *Self-Portrait of Marie Louise Elisabeth Vigée-Lebrun,* 1791. Oil on canvas, 39 x 31 7/8" (99 x 81 cm). © National Trust 1991/ Angelo Hornak.

Some artists paint pictures of their families.

Pictures B and C show a brother and sister.

Their first names are Louis and Marie.

Marie painted the portrait of her brother Louis.

Later, Marie painted her **self-portrait.**

You can create a portrait or self-portrait.

Who would you like to show? Why?

 Mino Da Fiesole, *Relief of a Woman,* ca. 1475–80, 13 3/16 x 11" (34 x 28 cm). Isabella Stewart Gardner Museum, Boston / Art Resource, New York.

Look at the **relief sculptures** in pictures A and B. Find shapes that stand out. Find shapes that go back. What else do you see?

 Unknown, *Head of Sassanian King Shapur II*, 200–600 A.D. Silver. The Metropolitan Museum of Art, New York (Fletcher Fund, 1965).

You can create a relief sculpture.

Make a sculpture of a face.

1. Plan and cut out shapes. Glue the shapes down.

2. Brush glue on your work. Press down some foil.

3. Add textures and details.

 Winslow Homer, *Snap the Whip,* 1872. Oil on canvas, 22 x 36" (56 x 92 cm). Butler Institute of American Art, Youngstown, Ohio.

Do you like to play outdoors with friends?
Can you show how you play in a picture?

Look at the artwork in picture A.
What are the people doing? How can you tell?
How do your arms and legs bend?

Student artwork.

Allan Rohan Crite, *Marble Players,* 1938. Oil on canvas, 25 x 30" (63 x 76 cm).
The Boston Athenaeum (Gift of the artist).

Look at picture C.

How does the artist show children playing?

Students made the artworks in picture D.

You can make artwork.

How can you show you are playing outdoors?

 Vincent Van Gogh, *Beach at Scheveningen,* 1882. Brush and watercolor heightened with gouache, 13 1/2 x 12 1/4" (35 x 51 cm). The Baltimore Museum of Art (The Cone Collection, formed by Dr. Claribel Cone and Miss Etta Cone of Baltimore, Maryland).

Where do you see a crowd of people?

How can you show a crowd?

Look at the artwork in picture A.

Some of the people look near to you.

Some of the people look far away.

Can you explain why?

 Student artwork.

Students created picture C.
They worked together to make it.
Which people look near? Why?
Which people look far away?

Draw different sizes of people.
Cut out the drawings.
Can you show people near to you?
Can you show people far away?

A Edouard Manet, *Flowers in a Crystal Vase,* 1882. Oil on canvas, 12 7/8" x 9 5/8" (33 X 24 cm). The Louvre Museum, Paris, © Photo R.M.N.

B Charles Demuth, *Tomatoes, Peppers and Zinnias*, ca. 1927. Watercolor, 17 5/8 x 11 1/2" (45 x 29 cm). Collection of the Newark Museum (Purchase 1948, Arthur F. Egner Memorial Fund).

What objects do you see in these three paintings?

Paintings about objects are called **still lifes.**

A still life shows objects that people like to see or use.

Why do you think artists make still life paintings?

C **Henri Fantin-Latour, _Still Life,_** 1866. Oil on linen canvas, 24 3/8 x 29 1/2" (62 x 75 cm). National Gallery of Art, Washington, DC (Chester Dale Collection).

Which paintings do you like?

Can you explain why you like them?

Create a picture of a still life.

Show objects you like to see or use.

Show how these objects look together.

 Henri Matisse, *The Thousand and One Nights*, 1950. Gouache on cut and pasted paper, 54 3/4 x 147 1/4" (139 x 374 cm). The Carnegie Museum of Art (Acquired through the generosity of the Sarah Mellon Scaife family, 71.23).

An artist cut out shapes for this collage.

The collage tells about a fairy tale.

What shapes do you see?

 a cave

 smoke

 magic lamps

 lightning

Do you have a favorite story?

What parts of the story are important?

Think of some shapes that help tell the story.

Cut out the shapes and paste them down.

This is one way to plan a collage.

 Khem Karan, *Prince Riding an Elephant,* Mughal, period of Akbar (1556-1605). Opaque watercolor and gold on paper. The Metropolitan Museum of Art (Rogers Fund, 1925).

Artists in many lands make pictures about animals.
An artist from India made this painting for a prince.

How does the artist show action or motion?
This painting has many **details,** too.
Details are small shapes, lines and patterns.
What do the details show?

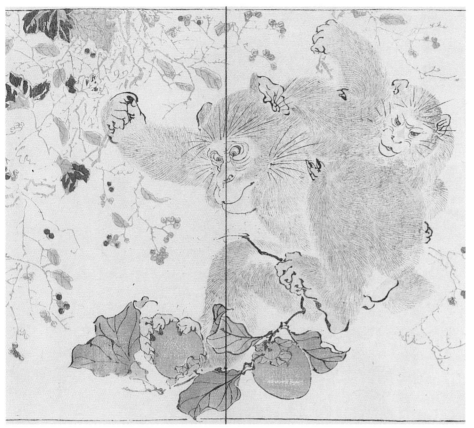

C Student artwork.

An artist from Japan created picture B.
Why did the artist use many details?
How did the artist show motion?

Create a picture of an animal that you like.
Show how it can move around.
What details will you show? Why?

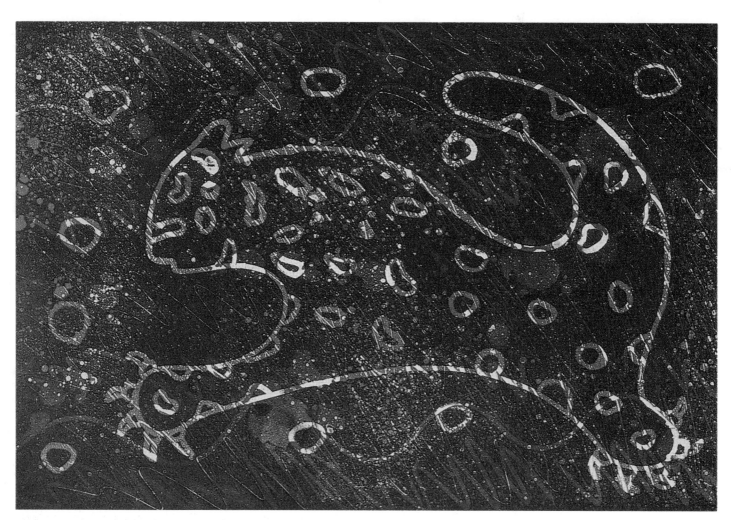

A   **Linda Lomahaftewa, *Jaguar,*** 1988. Monotype, 22 x 30" (56 x 76 cm). Courtesy of the artist.

This artist put ink on metal.

Then she drew a picture in the ink.

She put paper over the ink.

Her picture is a **monoprint.**

How did the artist show the motion of the animal?

What else do you see in her print?

You can make a monoprint.

1. Brush some thick paint.

2. Draw into the wet paint.
What tools can you use?

3. Put paper over the paint.
Gently rub the paper.

B   Student artwork.

C   Student artwork.

Amado Peña, *Los Pescados Peña.* 1978. Serigraph, 22 x 32" (56 x 81 cm). El Taller Gallery, Austin, Texas.

What colors, shapes and patterns do you see in picture A?
What helps you know the scene is **imaginary?**

Now look at the painting in picture B.
Some real fish have colors and patterns like these.
What else makes the painting look **realistic**?

Some creatures that live in water have unusual names. Imagine how they look.

sea horse
sea lion
sea cow
star fish
rabbit fish
cat fish

How could you find out how these creatures really look?

 Barbara Wallace, *Spots and Stripes,* 1987. Watercolor. ©1991 Barbara Wallace.

Create a picture of an underwater scene.
Will you show a realistic or imaginary scene?
What plants and animals will you show? How?

 Georgia O'Keeffe, *Poppy,* 1927. Oil on canvas, 30 x 36" (76 x 91 cm). Museum of Fine Arts, St. Petersburg, Florida (Gift of Charles C. and Margaret Stevenson Henderson in Memory of Jeanne Crawford Henderson).

Do you like to see things the way artists do?

Why does the poppy flower look so large?

What colors and shapes did the artist use?

What else did the artist want you to see?

Vincent Van Gogh, *Sunflowers,* 1887. Oil on canvas, 24 x 17" (61 x 43 cm). The Metropolitan Museum of Art (Rogers Fund).

This painting shows two large sunflowers.
What else did the artist want you to see?

Everything you see has a special look.
Find something you like to see in nature.
Draw it as large as you can.
Color your picture to show what you see.

 Bill Reid at work in his studio. Photograph: Rolf Bettner.

B **Bill Reid, *Raven Discovering Mankind in a Clamshell,*** 1970. Carved boxwood, 2 3/4 x 2 3/4 x 2" (7 x 7 x 6 cm). Canadian Museum of Civilization.

Bill Reid is a North American Indian.

His tribe is named Haida.

Bill Reid's ideas for art come from Haida stories.

In many Haida stories, animals are symbols for ideas.

Picture B shows a raven.

A raven is a Haida **symbol** for wisdom.

C   **Bill Reid, _Brooch with Eagle Design,_** 1970. Abalone, 22 carat gold, constructed, repoussé, set, 2 3/4 x 2" (7 x 5 cm). Canadian Museum of Civilization (Lent by M. Joan Chalmers, C.M.).

Make up a story or find one you like.
What symbols can you draw to share the story?

Sculpture has form.
Do you see the big **forms**?
Artists can make forms
tell a story.

What stories do these sculptures tell?

Kopapik Quqyarqyuk, *Owl and Owlets,* 1968. Stone, 14 x 17 x 9"
(35 x 44 x 23 cm). Reproduced by courtesy of the West Baffin Eskimo
Cooperative Limited, Cape Dorset, N.W.T., Canada.

C
John B. Flannagan, *Chimpanzee,*
1928. Granite, 10 3/4 x 6 3/4"
(27 x 17 cm). Collection of Whitney
Museum of American Art, New York.

You can make forms from clay.
You can make the forms into a sculpture.
Make your forms tell a story.

Sargent Johnson, *Forever Free,*
1933. Wood with lacquer on cloth,
36 x 11 1/2 x 9 1/2" (92 x 29 x 24 cm).
San Francisco Museum of Modern Art
(Gift of Mrs. E. D. Lederman).

Constantin Brancusi, *The Kiss,* 1912. Limestone,
23 x 13 x 10" (58 x 33 x 25 cm). Philadelphia Museum of Art
(The Louise and Walter Arensberg Collection).

 A **Kiawak Ashoona,** *Shaman.* Inuit Gallery of Vancouver. Photograph: Trevor Mills.

B **Oshweetok,** *Fisherwoman,* ca. 1963. Soapstone and ivory, 6 1/4 x 8 x 5" (16 x 20 x 12 cm). Reproduced by permission of the West Baffin Eskimo Co-operative Ltd., Cape Dorset, NWT, Canada.

Sculptures can tell us about people.

North American Indians who live in Canada created these artworks.

The artists live where it is cold.

The sculptures show people in warm clothing.

C Sarah Akisuk Alaku, *Woman Holding Bear Cub and Baby,* ca. 1967. Stone, 5 7/8 x 14 1/8 x 7 1/2″ (15 x 36 x 19 cm). Art Collection of the Toronto Dominion Bank.

Look closely.

What are the people doing?

Do you see big forms?

Where?

Do you see details? Why?

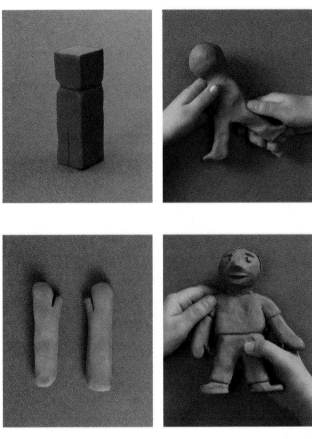

D

Make a sculpture in clay.

Show a person in clothes.

What details can you add?

Patterns and Clay
Sculptures Can Show Details

Sculptures can have patterns and textures.
Find the patterns and textures on this sculpture.

 Ceremonial covered vessel of the type huo, in the form of an elephant.
Shang, late An-yang, 11th century B.C., China. Bronze, 6 3/4 x 8 3/8 x 4 3/16" (17 x 21 x 11 cm). Courtesy of the Freer Gallery of Art, Smithsonian Institution, Washington, DC.

You can make
patterns in clay.

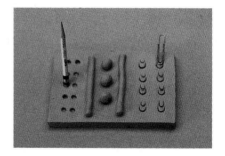

Find ways to
create textures.

Julio Gonzalez, *Head of Montserrat, Crying II (Cabeza Montserrat No. 2),* 1941-1942.
Bronze, 12 3/4 x 6 1/8 x 10 1/4" (32 x 16 x 26 cm). Hirshhorn Museum and Sculpture Garden,
Smithsonian Institution, Washington, DC (Gift of Joseph H. Hirshhorn, 1966). Photograph: Lee
Stalsworth.

What details do you see in pictures A and D?

Details are the small things you see.

Why did the artists create details?

The sun and moon are ideas in many artworks.

The sun helps plants grow.

The moon brings light at night .

James Bender, *Bella Coola Sun Mask.* Polychromed wood.
Photograph: Bob Bigford.

Unknown, *Mexican Sun Mask.* Paint on clay, 19" (48 cm).
Collection of Jo Miles Schumann.

The artworks in pictures A and B honor the sun.

A North American Indian carved the mask in picture A.

An artist from Mexico made the sculpture in picture B.

Many artists show the sun and moon as faces.
The mask in picture C shows a moon.
A North American Indian carved it from wood.

D Student artwork.

Joe Peters, *Moon Mask.* Courtesy of Granville Native Art,
Vancouver, British Columbia.

Students made relief sculptures.
They made parts stand out.
What other ideas did they use?

 Marvin Finn at work in his studio.
Photograph © 1989 Dan Dry.

B **Marvin Finn, *Bird With Tall Patterned Tail.*** Photograph © 1989 Dan Dry.

Mr. Finn is a sculptor.
He lives in Kentucky.
His kitchen is his studio.

Mr. Finn created the bird in picture B.
The wood is **assembled**, or glued together.
What patterns did he paint?

An artist from Brazil created the bird in picture C.

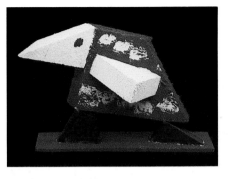

Student artwork.

Painted Scrap Wood Toy, Brazil, 20th century. Wood, paint, 7" (18 cm) high.
Collection of the Children's Museum, Indianapolis, Indiana. Photograph: Bradley Smith.

You can create sculpture.

Find some interesting forms.

Glue them together.

Paint them.

Your sculpture will be an assemblage.

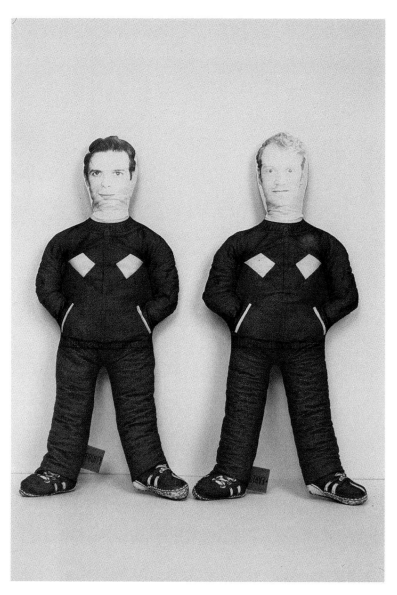

 Rob Pruitt and Jack Early, *Self-portraits of the Artists as Dolls,* 1991.
Heat transfer photographs on synthetic fiber, 32 x 12" (81 x 30 cm) each.
Courtesy of the 303 Gallery.

Sculptures are thick. They are not flat.

These sculptures are made from cloth.

These sculptures are self-portraits.

A self-portrait is a likeness of the artist.

Sculptures can be made to share a feeling. What feelings seem to go with these sculptures ? Why ?

C Create a sculpture.

Draw a thick body.
Cut around the edges.

 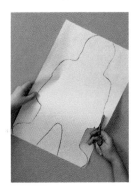

Trace the shape and cut it.

Close most of the edges.
Stuff paper inside.

B **Unknown,** ***Watchdog*** (detail of mosaic), pre A.D. 79. Mosaic. Collection, Museo Archeologico Nazionale, Naples.

A **Patricia J. Fay,** ***House.*** Marble wall piece, tile, 48 x 54" (122 x 137 cm). Courtesy of the artist.

The artwork in picture A is a **mosaic**.

The small pieces are thin stones, called tiles.

The tiles are placed side by side in cement.

The mosaic in picture B was made long ago in Pompeii, Italy.

The mosaic was near the door of a home.

Some mosaics had these words: "Beware of the dog."

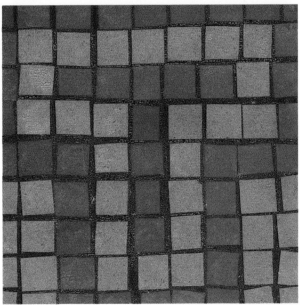

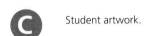
Student artwork.

Students created these
mosaics.
What designs did they make?
What colors did they use?

You can create a mosaic.
Cut some strips of paper.
Cut across the strips.

Glue each piece down.
Put the pieces side by side.

A

Mary T. Osceola, *Patchwork Jacket,* 1984. Cotton, rickrack, 31 x 65" (79 x 165 cm). Photograph: Bobby Hansson.

People in many lands have special clothing.

Look at the shirt in picture A. A North American Indian artist in Florida made it. What patterns do you see?

Look at picture B. Robes like this are worn for plays in Japan. What patterns do you see?

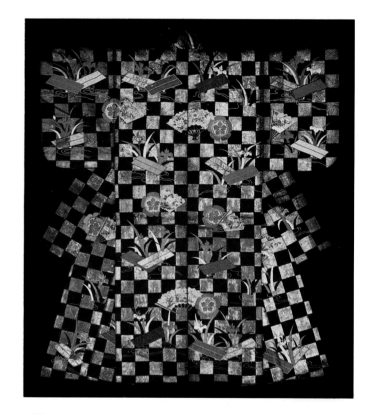

B

Nuihaku Noh Costume, Japanese, late 18th-early 19th century. Satin with silver check design. S.M. Nickerson Fund. Photograph by Christopher Gallagher. ©1992 The Art Institute of Chicago, All Rights Reserved.

 Teresa Sánchez Galindo, *Fringed Quechquemitl,* 20th century. Acrylic yarn woven in two webs on a backstrap loom, embroidered in cross stitch, 11 5/8 x 28" (29 x 71 cm). Collection of Chlöe Sayer. Photograph: David Lavender.

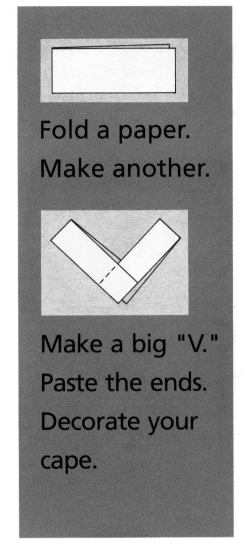

Fold a paper.
Make another.

Make a big "V."
Paste the ends.
Decorate your cape.

 D

A cape is worn over your shoulders.
An artist from Mexico created this cape.
What patterns do you see?

You can design a cape.
Students made the capes in picture E.

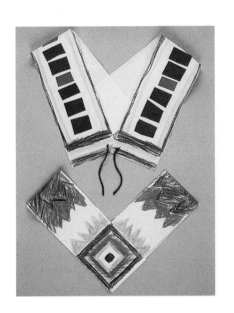

E

 Goat Sucker Birds, 3rd-2nd century B.C., Peru. Gold, 4 7/8" (13 cm) high. The Metropolitan Museum of Art (The Michael C. Rockefeller Memorial Collection, Bequest of Nelson A. Rockefeller, 1979). © 1991 The Metropolitan Museum of Art.

 Silver filigree hairpin, New Mexico, ca. 1880. Collection, Palace of the Governors, Santa Fe, New Mexico.

People in many lands make decorations. The bird shapes in picture A are like buttons.

The artwork in picture B is a hairpin.

These artworks have balanced designs.
The left sides and right sides are alike.
This kind of balance is called **symmetry.**

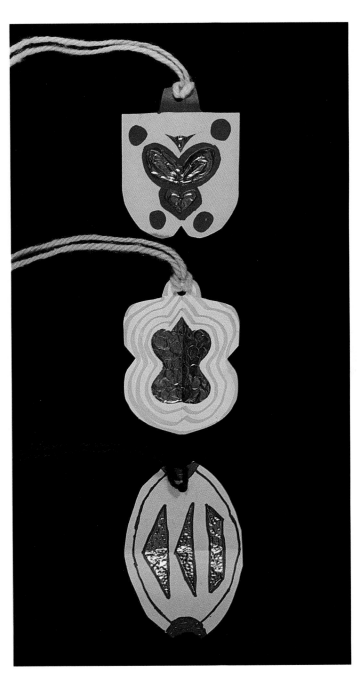

 Student artwork.

You can make decorations.
You can plan the balance.
You can plan the texture.

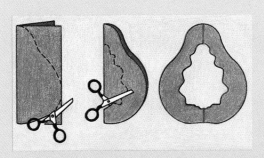

Fold a paper.
Cut the outside edges.
Cut into the fold.

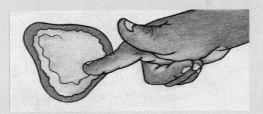

Glue foil on one side.

Turn your work over.
Put it on a soft pad.
Gently press the foil.

Many of the fabrics in your clothes are woven.
The tiny threads go over and under each other.

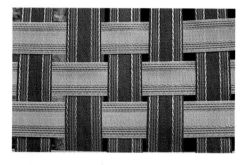

This chair is woven.
Wide strips go over and under.

Navajo weaver at work. Courtesy of Shostal Associates, New York. Photograph: Ray Manley.

This Navajo Indian woman is **weaving** a rug from yarn.
She is weaving on a **loom**.

You can weave paper.

 D

Fold your paper.
Cut it. This will
be your loom.

 E

Weave strips over
and under.
Can you create a
pattern?

You can be creative with weaving.

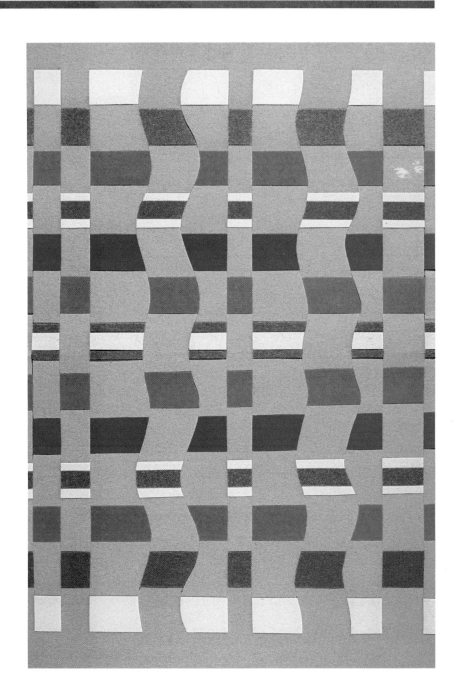

F Carol Hartsock, *Paper weaving.*

A   ***Indigo blue tie-dyed fabric,*** Togo, West Africa. From the collection of Mrs. Cyril Miles.

B   Detail of tie-dye fabric. Courtesy of Victoria Hughes.

Look at picture A.

An artist in Africa put **dye** on cloth.

Dye is a color that **stains** a cloth.

What patterns do the colors make?

The cloth in picture B was made in the United States.

What pattern do the colors make?

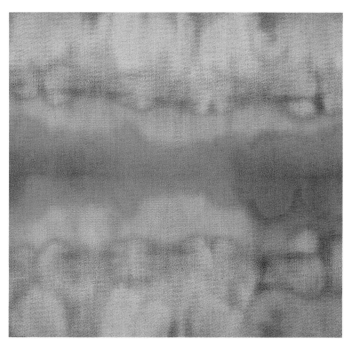

C   Student artwork.

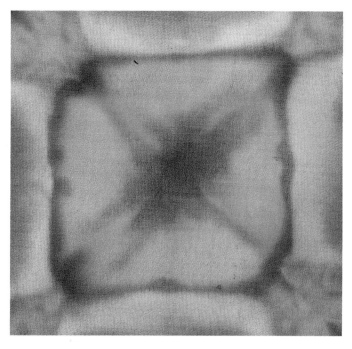

D   Student artwork.

Students put colors on folded cloth.

The colors stained the cloth in patterns.

You can make designs on cloth.

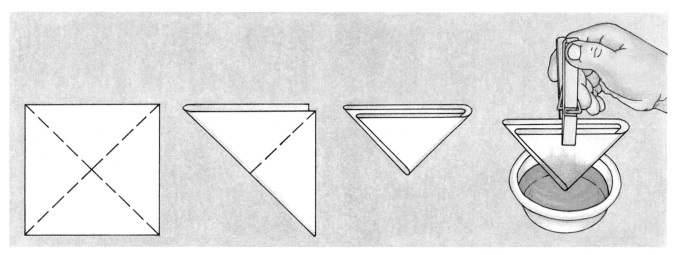

E

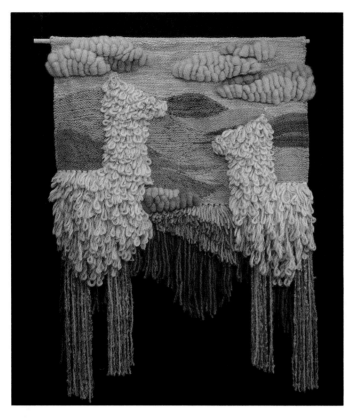

 Lori Kammeraad, *Llama,* 20th century, 44 x 60" (112 x 152 cm). Courtesy of the artist.

B ***Child's Wearing Blanket,*** ca. 1860–1870, Navajo. Native yarn and bayeta with cochineal, indigo and green dye, 38 1/2 x 60" (98 x 152 cm). Courtesy of Willis Henry Auctions, Inc.

Many artworks are made from cloth.

You can see and feel the textures in cloth.

Look at the weavings in pictures A and B.

How would each artwork feel if you touched it?

What patterns can you see?

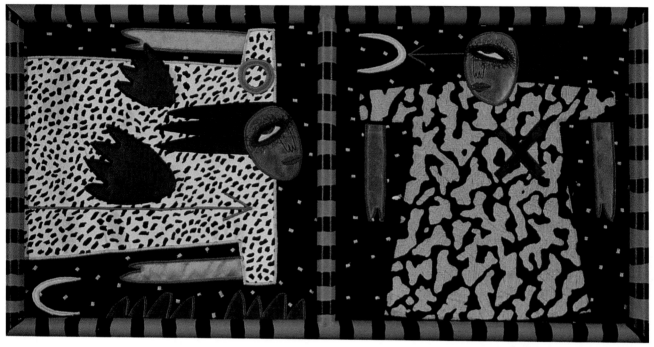

Chris Roberts-Antieau, *Flying Woman,* 1989. Fiber, appliqué, 16 x 24" (41 x 61 cm). Courtesy of the artist.

Picture C hangs on a wall. The artwork is like a collage. The artist sews pieces of cloth together. Do you see textures and patterns?

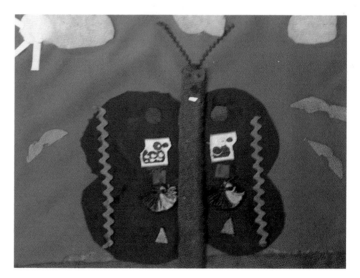

D Student artwork.

Students made wall hangings.

 Chinese New Year. Photograph: James Gray.

B Chinese New Year Banner. Photograph: James Gray.

Have you ever been in a parade?

What kinds of art can you see in a parade?

The woman in picture A is in a parade.

This parade is held to celebrate the Chinese New Year.

The **banner** in picture B was carried in the parade.

C Photograph: Cincinnati Recreation Banner project.

Children in Cincinnati, Ohio made banners.
They celebrated the joy of making art.

Your class can create banners and have a parade.
What would you like to celebrate?
How will you design your banners?

A ***Deep dish (brasero),*** decorated with motifs of palmette tree, pseudo-kufic and spiral designs, Spanish (Hispano-Moresque), ca. 1430. Earthenware, glazed, stain- and lustre-painted, 17 3/4" (45 cm) diameter. The Metropolitan Museum of Art (The Cloisters Collection, 1956).

Some artists create things for people to use. The plate in picture A was made long ago in Spain. The design has **radial** balance.

A radial design looks like a star or a wheel.
The main lines and shapes go out from the center.

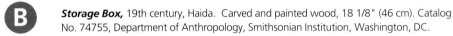

Storage Box, 19th century, Haida. Carved and painted wood, 18 1/8" (46 cm). Catalog No. 74755, Department of Anthropology, Smithsonian Institution, Washington, DC.

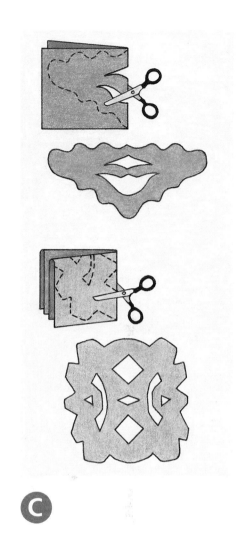

C

A North American Indian made this box.
It was used to store clothing.

The design on the front of the box has **symmetrical** balance. The lines and shapes are alike on both sides.

Create a design on a box, cup or plate.
Cut radial or symmetrical shapes for your design.

D Student artwork.

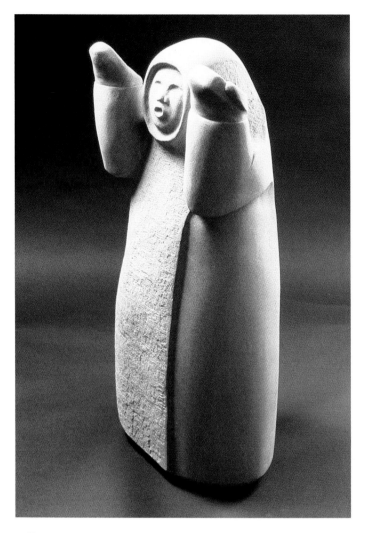

A **Sue Bevins-Ericsen,** ***Even the Rocks Cry Out,*** 1983.
Sandstone, 38 x 14 x 12 " (97 x 36 x 30 cm). Courtesy of the
artist.

B **Jim Hart,** ***Dogfish Mask,*** Haida,1981. Red cedar, paint, 12
1/4 x 9 1/2 " (31 x 24 cm). Photograph: Bobby Hansson.

Artworks help people remember the past.

North American Indians created these artworks.

Each artist's work means something special.

Your teacher will tell you about each artwork.

Look at each picture and listen carefully.

Then tell what you think each artwork means.

What do you like to remember?

Can you make an artwork to remember the past?

 Fred Brown in his studio. Work shown: **The Piano Players** from his *Blues Series.* Courtesy of Ken Barboza Associates.

Do you know people who create art?

What kinds of art do they make?

Look at the four pictures of artists.

What kinds of art do they make?

What jobs, or **art careers,** do they have?

D Jewelry maker at work. Photograph: John Senzer for the Fashion Institute of Technology.

C Monique Cliche-Spénard. National Museums of Canada, Ottawa. Photograph: Rolf Bettner.

Look again. Who creates large paintings?

Which artist prints a picture on paper?

Who makes jewelry from metal?

Which artist sews quilts from cloth?

Look for art in your world.

What kinds of art do you see?

How did artists help to make it?

 Child's Roller Skates. Courtesy of Fisher Price, Inc.

 Dust Pan/Brush Pack. Designer: Robert Staubitz, Group Four Design. Courtesy of Kellogg Brush Company.

You see art at home and at school.
Artists plan many things people use.

Look at the design of each object.
Artists planned the colors and forms.
Artists chose the textures and materials.
What else did the **designers** plan?

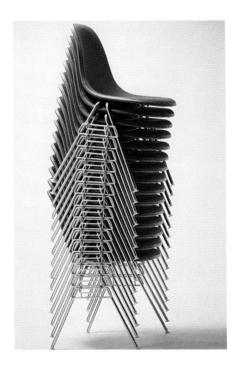

Charles Eames, *Stacking chairs on steel rod legs,* *ca. 1950.* Courtesy of Herman Miller, Inc.

Shoprite, Yonkers, New York. Design: Planned Expansion Group. Courtesy of Retail Reporting Corporation.

Artists design packages for stores.

They plan the shelves and racks.

Everything must fit together.

What else must a designer think about?

What objects in your classroom did an artist design?

Tell what you think about the design of each object.

A Fruit Works store at Mill Creek. Q-5 Design, Wayne, New Jersey. Courtesy of Retail Reporting Corporation.

B Designer: Lynn Phelps. Illustrator: Daniel Craig. *Minnesota Guide,* published by *The Minneapolis Star Tribune,* 1987.

Art is all around you.

You see art on signs.

You see art in newspapers.

Artists design the letters.

They design the pictures too.

They make letters and pictures fit together.

 Darrel Milsap, *The Hip Place To Go,* 1982. Courtesy of The Zoological Society of San Diego and Phillips Ramsey, San Diego, California.

 Gail Stampar, *Tyler Spring Crafts Fair,* 1987. Silkscreen poster with pinwheel. Craft Association of Tyler.

Look at picture C.

It is a large outdoor sign.

What does the picture tell you?

What do the words say?

Look at picture D.

What do you see first?

What else does the artist say?

How does the design help?

 Carl Zahn, *Matisse exhibition, subway car card,* 1966. 11 x 28" (28 x 71 cm). Courtesy of the artist.

Some artists design **letters** of the alphabet.

They use the letters to create art.

They create art to share ideas.

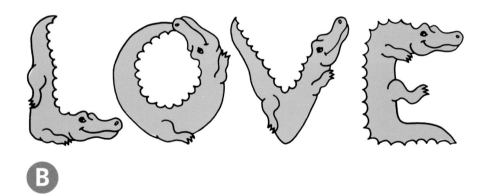

B

Some artists like to draw funny letters.

They use their imaginations.

 Student artwork.

You can create art with letters.

You can cut letters from paper.

You can draw and decorate letters.

What ideas for art do you have?

A Illustration from *Tigress* by Helen Cowcher. ©1991 Helen Cowcher. Reprinted by permission of Farrar, Straus, and Giroux, Inc.

Artists create pictures for books.

These artists are illustrators.

This book tells a story from Africa.

Find a picture book you like.

Tell why you like the illustrations.

She leaves the sanctuary and pads silently through thornbushes, into the forbidden lands beyond. Again, monkeys' urgent, shrill voices fill the air.

As dawn breaks, they reach the sanctuary. All is quiet and they can rest.

Beyond the sanctuary's border, the scent of camel and goat still wafts in the air. The tigress twitches her nose, then sleeps.

What do these pictures tell you?
How can you illustrate a story?

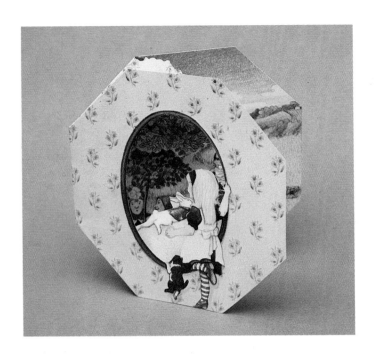

 A   *Greeting card,* Alice in Wonderland theme. © DoDo Designs, England.

B   *Trade Card: Correct Your Sight,* 19th century. Courtesy of the New York Historical Society, New York City.

These cards send messages.
What parts did artists design?

Which designs look very old?
Why do you think so?

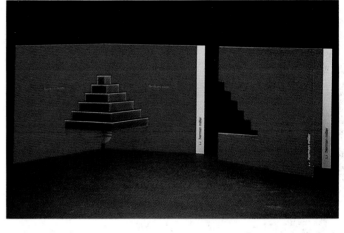

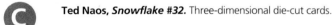

C
Ted Naos, *Snowflake #32.* Three-dimensional die-cut cards.

D
Season's Greetings. Design: Telment Design Associates.

These cards have forms.
Forms stand up or out.
Some forms have holes.
You can see through holes.

Send a message on a card.
Make your card have forms.

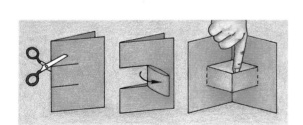

Cut.   Fold.   Press out.

Find these shapes
in the big picture
of the house.

C

A

Point to the large
and small squares.

D

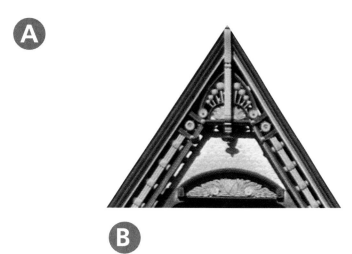

B

Find tall and wide
rectangles.

Look for these
two triangles.

E

Find some patterns.
Patterns have repeated
lines and shapes.

Are there old houses in your town? Do some of them look like this? Draw a picture of a house. What shapes and patterns will you draw?

Carson House, ca. 1886, Eureka, California.

An **architect** is an artist who plans buildings.

Some architects design homes where people live.

A Philip Johnson, *Wiley House*, 1952-1953.

This home has one main form.
The form is like a cube.

B

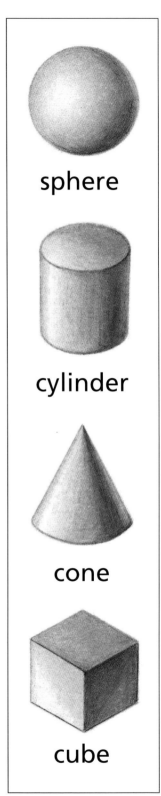

sphere

cylinder

cone

cube

C

Look at this house.

Do you see the cone and the cylinder?
Why do buildings have forms?

E

Make a **model** of a house.
Find and make some forms.

These are forms.

Make forms. Use paper.

Cut, fold and paste.

F

117

Architects plan buildings that people like to see.

They plan buildings that people like to use.

They design many kinds of buildings.

 David Johnston, *Markham Fire Hall No. 1,* Ontario, Canada. Photograph courtesy of the architect.

An architect designed this fire station. How is it used? Do you like the design? Why or why not?

 Michael Graves, *Public Services Building,* 1982. Portland, Oregon. Photograph courtesy of Tom Clark Architectural Associates.

This is an office building. What parts have been planned? How do people use it?

A city has many kinds of buildings.

Think of a building you want to design.

Draw the big shapes first. What else can you add?

Beverly Willis Architects, Inc. *Margaret Hayward Playground Building,* San Francisco Parks and Recreation Department, 1979. Architects: Beverly Willis Architects, Inc., New York and San Francisco. Photograph: Michael Kanouff.

Sunkist Plaza, Markham, Ontario, Canada. Courtesy of Stone Kohn McQuire Vogt Architects.

This is a playground building. Why are playgrounds good to have?

This is a place to go shopping. An architect designed it. What parts are planned?

Courtesy of Edward Makauskas Architect, Inc., Ontario, Canada.

Do you like this design for a library?
What parts did an artist plan?

Indoor spaces are called **interiors.**
Artists who plan rooms are called interior designers.
Interior designers choose colors for walls.
They choose carpets, chairs and curtains.
They decide where everything is placed in a room.

(B) *Georgian Bay Cottage,* Perry Sound, Canada. Courtesy of Stark, Hicks, Spragge, Architects, Ontario, Canada.

Design a make-believe room you would like.

Draw the windows, doors and walls.

What furniture will be in your room?

Choose colors, shapes and patterns you like.

Your drawing will be an interior design.

Louis Comfort Tiffany, *View of Oyster Bay.* From the McKean Collection, on extended loan to The Metropolitan Museum of Art. Courtesy of the Charles Hosmer Morse Museum of American Art, Winter Park, Florida.

This artwork is a window made from **stained glass.**
Metal strips hold the pieces of glass. When light comes
through the window, the colored glass glows.
Have you seen art like this? Where?

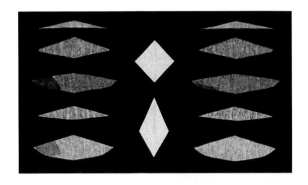

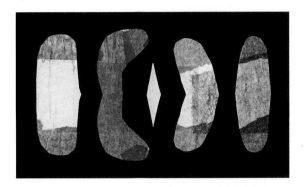

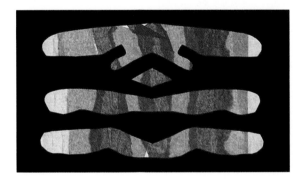

 Student artwork.

Students made designs to hang in a window.
You can explore light and color too.

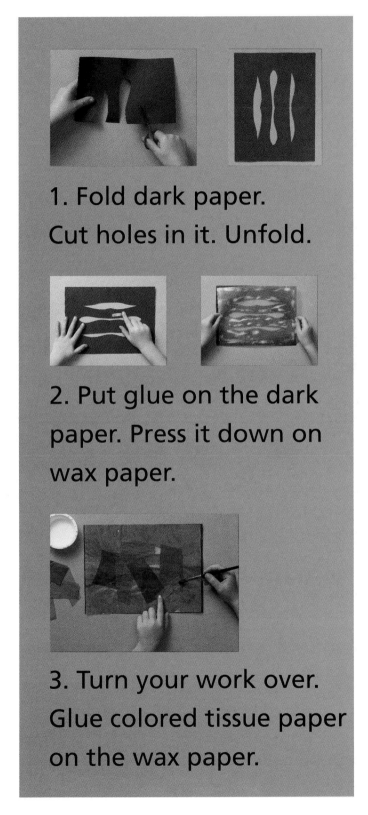

1. Fold dark paper. Cut holes in it. Unfold.

2. Put glue on the dark paper. Press it down on wax paper.

3. Turn your work over. Glue colored tissue paper on the wax paper.

C

 Moon Gate. View of traditional Chinese garden, Sung dynasty, 960–1279.

People in many lands create parks and gardens.

This park was built long ago in China.

It has a pond with water lilies. What else do you see?

The Glencoe Golf and Country Clubhouse, Calgary, Alberta, Canada. Architect: Boucock Craig and Partners.

Artists who plan parks and gardens are **landscape designers.**
Look at the garden in picture B. What parts were designed?

You can create a landscape design. How will your park or garden look?

 Student artwork.

Students created this design.

Look for old and new buildings in your town.
How are they alike? How are they different?

 Padre Antonio Peyri, *San Luis Rey Mission,* ca. 1811. California.

This church in California has a tower with bells. It has curves on part of the roof. It was designed by Spanish people who came to North America.

 William Strickland, *Independence Hall,* 1731–1791, Philadelphia, Pennsylvania.

This building helps people in the United States remember their history. It has a tall tower and spire. It was designed by English people who came to North America.

Frank Lloyd Wright, *Exterior of Solomon R. Guggenheim Museum,* 1959, New York City.

Some buildings are new. They have new materials and new forms. The ideas for designs are new.

The building in picture C has round forms. It is an art museum. It is made of concrete.

D *Sears Tower,* Chicago, Illinois, 1970–1974. Skidmore, Owings and Merrill Architects.

The building in picture D is very tall. It has 110 floors. It is a **skyscraper** made of steel and glass.

 William Henry Fox Talbot, *Photogenic Drawings of a Leaf,* ca. 1836-39. The Fox Talbot Museum, England.

Artworks can be **photographs.**

Photo means light. Graph means record.

Photographs are records made by light.

An artist made these photographs.

Why are there two pictures?

How are they alike?

How are they different?

B Student artwork.

C Student artwork.

D Student artwork.

Students made these pictures on a photocopy machine.

The machine has a strong light.

How can you create a photograph?

What will make it an artwork?

129

Art can be pictures of moving things.
Have you seen motion pictures?

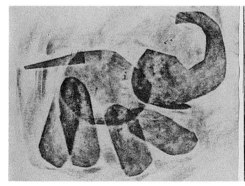

A

Does the pig seem to run? Why?

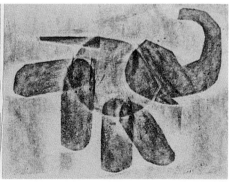

B Student artwork.

Students made pictures that seem to
move. How did they make pictures
that show motion?

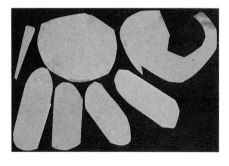

C

Pictures can seem to show motion.

This is how you see motion on television.

This is how you see motion in a movie.

D Student artwork.

A Robert Rauschenberg setting up an exhibition of his work.

The artist in picture A is having an **art show**.

He is choosing his best artwork for the show.

His show is in an **art gallery**.

Have you ever visited an art gallery?

Your class can plan an art show.

Choose your best artwork.

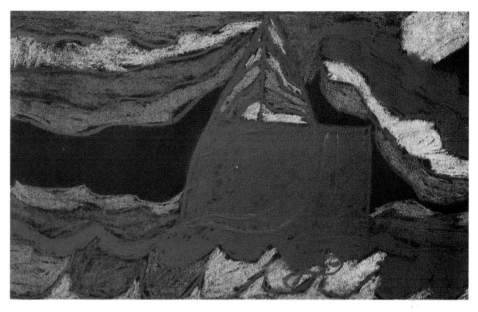

Students created the artworks on this page.

What makes each artwork special?

Art Safety

Study the pictures to learn safety rules.
Listen for other rules your teacher gives you.

1. Use all tools carefully. Keep art materials away from your eyes, mouth and face.

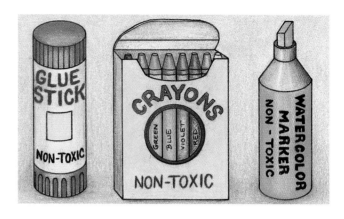

2. The labels on your art materials should say nontoxic. Nontoxic means the material is safe to use.

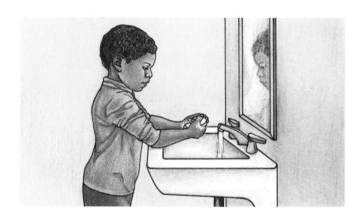

3. Wash your hands after art lessons. This step is needed if your hands are not clean.

4. If you spill something, help to clean it up. If a floor is wet, people can slip and fall.

You Can Help

Study the pictures to learn how to help.
What other things can you do to help?

1. Help everyone get ready for art.

2. Share materials. Save things you can use again.

3. Help to clean up and put art materials away.

4. Listen and think about what people say.

5. Talk about what you learn. Share what you know.

6. Save your art so you can see what you learn.

Artists and Artworks

Artists and Artworks

Picture Glossary

architect
page 116

art show
page 132

artist
page 6

assemble
page 80

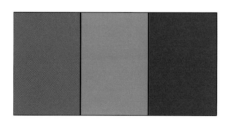
banners
page 96

brushstrokes
page 35

collage
page 13

cool colors
page 43

details
page 62

diagonal lines
page 49

forms
page 72

imaginary
page 66

interior
page 120

landscape
page 36

letters
page 108

lines
page 8

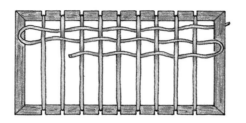

loom
page 90

monoprint
page 64

mosaic
page 84

motion lines
page 10

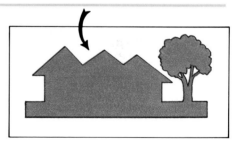

negative shape
page 22

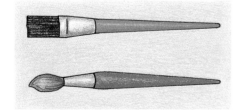

paintbrushes
page 34

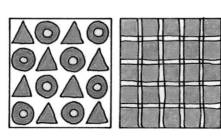

patterns
page 20

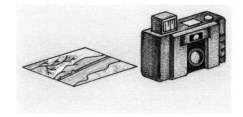

photograph
page 8

Picture Glossary

portrait
page 50

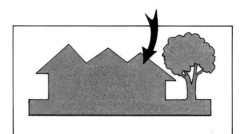

positive shape
page 22

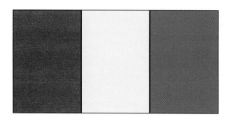

primary colors
page 30

print
page 20

radial balance
page 98

relief sculpture
page 52

sculpture
page 72

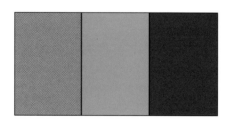

secondary colors
page 30

self-portrait
page 51

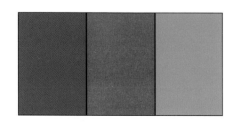

shades
page 44

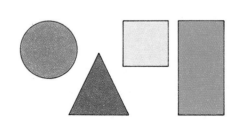

shapes
page 12

sketches
page 38

skyscrapers
page 127

stain
page 92

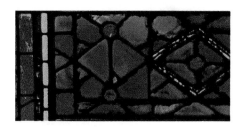

stained glass
page 122

stencil
page 24

still life
page 58

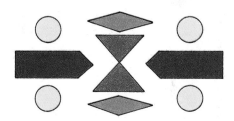

symmetry
page 88

texture
page 14

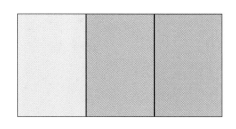

tints
page 45

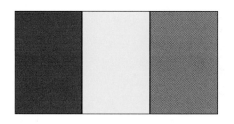

warm colors
page 42

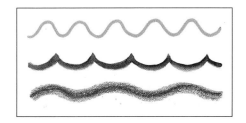

wavy lines
page 8

weaving
page 90

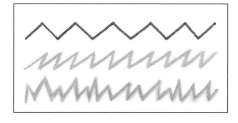

zigzag lines
page 8

Index